TEACH YOUR DOG TO READ
(for real)

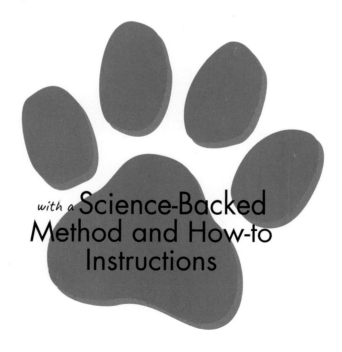

with a Science-Backed Method and How-to Instructions

Susan Holt Simpson

& Bernardo França

How to Use This Flipbook to Teach Your Dog to Read

You might be wondering, "Can I really teach my dog to read?"

It's a well-known fact that dogs can discriminate and respond to shapes. A consistent sequence of shapes—known as a word—is no different. In fact, training your dog in this new area of thinking will strengthen the pet-parent bond and increase your canine companion's capacity for problem solving and intelligence. You and your family dog have nothing to lose and so much to gain. Let's get started.

Plan well, then jump in!

Teaching your pet to read should be a fun and joyful experience. Set yourself up for success by storing your flipbook with high-value treats. Call your dog, then reveal the treats and the flipbook at the same time. Let your own enthusiasm show and use a repeatable invitation like, "Let's read!"

Whenever you teach something new to a human child or a fur baby, it's best to begin with the familiar. Choose three to five commands that they already know and obey well. From among that small group of words, select the one your dog has mastered at the highest level. For example: DOWN.

Prepare a training area by eliminating distractions such as other pets, toys, or persons. Stand in front of your furry buddy, holding the flipbook and a treat to keep your pet's attention. Flip the page to reveal the chosen command—the dog will see the large word alone in high contrast on a white page, and you will see the colorful illustration—and calmly say, "Down."

Celebrate with horns and balloons every time your fur baby gets even close to your desired behavior. Well . . . maybe no horns or balloons, but excitement-infused cuddles and compliments are a must.

Gradually extinguish your verbal command by softening your voice until you eventually only flip the page and wait for your canine companion to recognize the word and follow the command. Reading instruction requires patient repetition and enthusiastic reinforcement—you've got this!

When your literary pup achieves comfortable and swift recognition of the first word, choose a second one. Select a word that looks as different as possible in length or shape from the first. Repeat the steps—show the card, speak the command aloud, and joyfully reward the correct behavior. Gradually extinguish the verbal command and allow your fur pal to respond only to the word on the page. Keep reading sessions short and only continue as long as your pet is happily engaged in learning.

Where do you go from here?

What about all those other words? Future training sessions! As your family dog learns new commands, pair them with the flipbook words. With consistent training, plenty of patience, and happy rewards, you and your scholarly pooch will be on the way to communicating at a whole new level.

Research has shown that dogs are capable of reading up to 20 words. Choose from the ones included, or consider training your dog to read assistance words found in public places, such as STOP, EXIT, and RESTROOM. Maybe you've wanted to add agility training to your pet's exercise routine—and yours too. Train your eager pup to read agility commands like TUNNEL, SEESAW, and WEAVE. Enrich your pet pal's reading experience by sharing it with a child who's also new to reading. Reading therapy organizations pair dogs and early readers to the great benefit of both.

Expanded canine intelligence and deeper pet-parent bonds are straight ahead. Let your fur buddy set the pace and enjoy an incredible experience with your literary pup.

Sources

"Concept Training: Shape Discrimination." Karen Pryor Academy. November 25, 2020. Accessed November 12, 2021. https://karenpryoracademy.com/concept-training-shape-discrimination/.

Puotinen, CJ. "Teaching Your Dog to Read." *Whole Dog Journal*. April 22, 2019. Accessed November 12, 2021. https://www.whole-dog-journal.com/training/teaching-your-dog-to-read/.

Drake, Pat. "Can Dogs Read? - Wag!" *WagWalking*. May 29, 2018. Accessed November 12, 2021. https://wagwalking.com/sense/can-dogs-read.

Staff, AKC. "Agility Tips: A Champion's Words to Train By." *American Kennel Club*. July 01, 2021. Accessed November 12, 2021. https://www.akc.org/expert-advice/training/agility-tips-a-champions-words-to-train-by/.

"Can Animals Read?" *Wonderopolis*. Accessed November 12, 2021. https://wonderopolis.org/wonder/can-animals-read.

Waugh, Rob. "Apes 'can Recognise the Written Word' - and Even Make Plans for the Future." *Daily Mail Online*. June 25, 2012. Accessed November 12, 2021. https://www.dailymail.co.uk/sciencetech/article-2164328/Apes-recognise-written-word--make-plans-future.html.

About Familius

Visit Our Website: www.familius.com

Familius is a global trade publishing company that publishes books and other content to help families be happy. We believe that the family is the fundamental unit of society and that happy families are the foundation of a happy life. We recognize that every family looks different, and we passionately believe in helping all families find greater joy. To that end, we publish books for children and adults that invite families to live the Familius Ten Habits of Happy Family Life: *love together, play together, learn together, work together, talk together, heal together, read together, eat together, give together*, and *laugh together*. Founded in 2012, Familius is located in Sanger, California.

Connect

Facebook: www.facebook.com/familiustalk

Twitter: @familiustalk, @paterfamilius1

Pinterest: www.pinterest.com/familius

Instagram: @familiustalk

FAMILIUS

BED

bed

STRETCH

stretch

LEASH

leash

WALK

walk

BALL

ball

CATCH

catch

BOWL

bowl

EAT

eat

WINDOW

window

CAT

cat

YAWN

yawn

COUCH

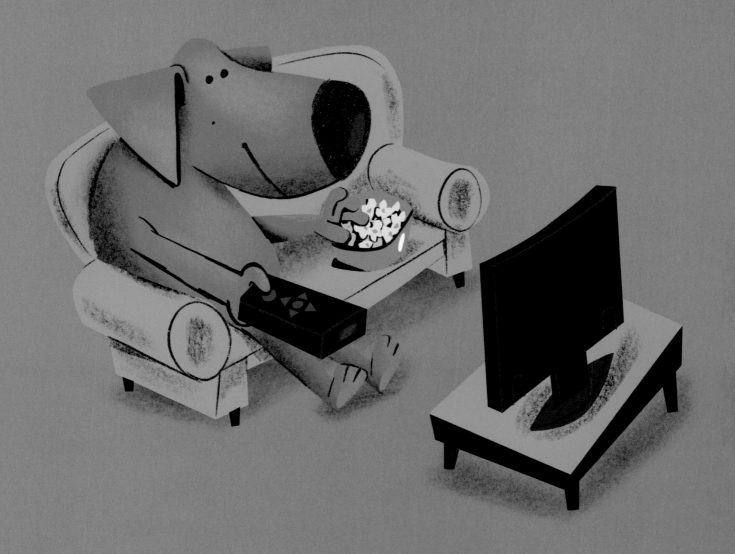

couch

WAIT

wait

PARK

park

RUN

run

TREAT

treat

SIT

sit

DOWN

down

SPIN

spin

SPEAK

speak

QUIET

quiet

BONE

bone

CLEAN

clean

BATH

bath

HIGH-FIVE

high-five

BOOK

book

ROLL

OVER

roll over

KISS

kiss

SLEEP

sleep

GOOD
DOG

good dog

Published by Familius LLC, www.familius.com

PO Box 1249, Reedley, CA 93654

Familius books are available at special discounts for bulk purchases, whether for sales promotions or for family or corporate use. For more information, contact Familius Sales at orders@familius.com.

Library of Congress Control Number: 2022937118

ISBN 978-1-64170-733-6

Printed in China

Edited by Peg Sandkam

Cover and book design by Brooke Jorden

10 9 8 7 6 5 4 3 2 1

First Edition